A CHAMPION SPEAKS

A Champion Speaks

ENIOLA OYEGUNLE

CONTENTS

Dedication

I dedicate this to you, son. You are so relentless and determined. You have inspired strength in me to face any obstacle. I have learnt from you how to be bold, and now I can tell a part of your story. I look forward to the day you will continue this story in your writing and show the world what is possible.

I also dedicate this to all children whom the world, in its efforts to understand their uniqueness, labels as "special," "autistic," or "neuro-divergent." You all can achieve great things despite these labels.

Finally, to parents and carers, I encourage you to be relentless in nurturing the best in your child. Whether or not your child eventually overcomes what looks to the world as a limitation, be persistent in making that child the best version of themselves.

Acknowledgements

I am grateful to God, the Father of my Lord Jesus Christ, for making this journey possible. I cried too many times to You, my Lord, concerning this son You gave me, and You answered me. You kept reminding me that You created him in Your image, and so You put good in him. Thank You for letting all the good You put in my son come to light. Every progress made is because You showed us the way and gave us the ability and grace to forge ahead. There will be no "champion" without you. My faith in God helped me not to lose my mind and gave me staying power all through the challenges. You assured me, dear Lord, that the outcome of my son's life is good. This remains my hope, and for this, I unapologetically say thank You, Lord.

Finally, my appreciation goes out to my son's nannies, teachers, doctors, healthcare professionals, education practitioners, therapists, and one-on-one support at his different schools, family, and friends who knew about my son's journey and encouraged us. We did not get here alone; we had a lot of help. I will provide a recollection of events from memory but with names changed to protect the privacy of those mentioned. I believe God led these people to us. I drew strength from them along the way, as did my son, and I will forever be grateful for this. The journey continues still, but we face it with confidence. The past almost ten years have shown me that greatness lies ahead for my son. Thank you in advance to those who will stick with us as my son continues his journey beyond the label.

Introduction

Your responsibility as a parent begins when your child is handed over to you after birth. The challenges that come with parenting a child are rarely discussed. We tend to focus on the joys of parenthood, but beneath the surface lies a world of unspoken struggles, fears, and doubts that parents often face alone. Every child brings their own unique needs, and every parent feels the weight of the responsibility to support them through it all.

As a parent, you anticipate each developmental milestone, expecting them to come naturally. You rarely consider the possibility of delays, especially in something as fundamental as speech. The journey to finding a solution to your child's developmental delays can feel lonely and lead to unexpected discoveries. In a race against time, questions arise that you don't easily find answers to, as well as dealing with intense emotions while trying to make sense of a reality you are unprepared for.

A few months before my son's birthday, I found myself reflecting on his journey so far. Every child has the potential to thrive with the right support from their parents and carers. This book seeks to inspire parents and carers by presenting detailed accounts of my experience raising my son, including some of the lessons learnt. The path to hearing my son speak was not straightforward but was one filled with unexpected challenges, countless tears, and a mix of guilt and self-blame, wondering if perhaps I had done something wrong. Over time, I learned to turn those tears into resilience. Today, I can proudly say, "A champion speaks."

My introductory letter to my son

My dear son,

I will never stop thanking God for the gift of your birth. You were born in December 2014. I call you my all-in-one-year testimony, as your conception and birth happened in the same year. Your Dad and I were born and raised in Nigeria, West Africa. We are both from the Yoruba tribe, which is in the southwestern part of Nigeria. We lived in Lagos, which is also in the southwestern part of Nigeria. When we thought of names to give you, your dad wanted us to call you Champion. I was not entirely convinced about how we would call a Nigerian boy from the Yoruba tribe Champion. We, however, set out to look for an English equivalent known name and then found a perfect name to call you. You have other Nigerian Yoruba names which have resonated strongly with your journey:

- Oluwasegun, meaning "God is victorious," is given to you by your Dad.
- Oluwabamise, meaning "God helped me do it," is a name I gave you.
- Opemipo, meaning "My thankfulness is plenty," is given to you by my Mum.
- Oluwaseun, meaning "Thank God" or "God has done something," is given to you by my Mum.
- Iyanuoluwa, meaning "The wonder of God," is given to you by your Dad's Mum.
- Abiodun, meaning "Born during a festival" (as you were born close to Christmas), is given to you by your Dad's Mum.

- Oluwatobiloba, meaning "God is great," is given to you by my aunt Sage.

Now, my dear son, I will try to share my experiences of raising you up to almost ten years old.

PART 1

My experiences from my son's birth till his tenth year

| 1 |

The Beginning (from age 0-2)

Oh, what a trying pregnancy! I had severe pains a lot of the time due to degenerating fibroids. Before this pregnancy, I never knew I had fibroids, so you can imagine my shock at my first scan when I was told that I had multiple fibroids. From early on in my pregnancy, I could only sleep on a couch till after I had my son. I was so determined that this son of mine would be born outside Nigeria, and thankfully, my husband supported the decision. The challenges I had throughout my pregnancy strengthened my resolve to access the best care possible, no matter the cost.

My son was born a month before his scheduled due date because I had severe seizures, which made me unconscious. This was one of the symptoms associated with pre-eclampsia, which came on suddenly as I never even knew I was at risk of such a condition. My blood pressure spiked, which caused the seizures, and the only option was to have my son delivered. I do not recall much of what happened as I was unconscious, but I remain glad that we survived the ordeal. I am grateful to my cousin and his family, the ambulance and emergency teams who swiftly responded to me at Holy Cross Hospital Maryland, USA, where my son was born.

My son spent his first ten days in the neonatal intensive care unit (NICU) due to his early birth. There were no complications, so once he started feeding well from the bottle, we were discharged and free to go live our lives. We spent some time in the US to recover well. Thankfully, I received help from my Mum and Aunt Sage throughout our time in the US. I really would have been clueless without them. A few months after my son's birth, I returned to Nigeria, ready to raise him alongside his Dad. He achieved all the regular milestones of sitting, crawling, walking, and even what I thought was babbling, so I felt no reason to worry.

We celebrated my son's one-year-old birthday with much fanfare in Lagos, Nigeria. As the firstborn, we threw him a party with family and friends. As a typical one-year-old, the party was more for us as he could not be bothered to enjoy any part of it. We managed to take him pictures, though, thankfully. My husband and I were responsible for my son's care at home. We were supported by a nanny who was hired to cover daytime hours, so three of us served as my son's caregivers. As we approached his two-year birthday, I started worrying that he was not talking much. He habitually pulled us by the hand to help him get things he wanted, like water. I checked Google to understand this speech delay, and stories like "boys speak late", "every child is different", etc. kept me somewhat sane. Also, people advised that as he was the only child at home, we should enrol him in school early so he could mix with other children and learn to talk. He started attending a nursery school in Lagos, Nigeria, when he turned about 18 months old.

I was still quite concerned after his second birthday as all we were getting as the speech was sounds but no words spoken with clarity: no mummy or Mum or Mama. Even Dada, which was supposed to be easier to pronounce, was non-existent. I often raised this concern with my husband, but we were both clueless about what we could do. Regarding my son responding to his name, we were still unsure as sometimes it felt like he did, and other times it felt like he didn't. We talked to him frequently, and it almost felt like he didn't hear us. It felt like he was in his world and didn't want to be bothered. My son was such a happy child, always smiling, loved hugs, cuddles, tickles, and the like. He was also very active throughout this time and could not sit still. He was so curious and always touching things that looked attractive. He had a hot water accident in school; as we were told, he curiously went to play with a bowl of water and unknowingly spilt hot water all over himself. This was such a traumatic experience. I was at work that day and got a call from my son's school that he was rushed to the hospital. I hurriedly drove for about thirty minutes from my office in Ikeja to Ikoyi Lagos, where the hospital was. Thankfully, he recovered well, but I knew his days in that school were numbered.

A few months after his second birthday, we saw a doctor after he had flu-like symptoms. The doctor asked about his general well-being, and I mentioned his speech delay. She referred us to an Ear, nose, and throat (ENT) specialist to at least check his hearing, as she could tell I was concerned. My Mum had to take my son to the appointment with the ENT specialist as I had to go to work. She later called to inform me that the diagnosis was that my son was tongue-tied, and minor surgery was required to correct it. I was distraught and literally in tears, not knowing what that meant. My Mum further mentioned that the specialist said my son might be mildly autistic due to the way he was uneasy and restless during the appointment.

At this time, I didn't know much about autism, not even sure I had heard the word before. Not too long after the evaluation by the ENT specialist, my son was scheduled for a mini procedure to correct the tongue tie. He recovered smoothly from the procedure. Shortly after this procedure, we noticed his sounds becoming clearer. We could hear him attempting to recite the alphabet, count from 1 to 10, etc. He was so attached to his tablet computer and listened to many nursery rhymes. We could now hear with some clarity sounds he mimicked from the lyrics of the nursery rhymes he listened to.

I was still deeply troubled by the ENT specialist's evaluation of my son, especially the suggestion of autism. I could not get my mind off the supposed autism diagnosis. In my mind, I was like, how can a specialist state such after just a short time of evaluating my son's ear, nose, and throat? However, I was wise enough to start reading up on autism, i.e., understanding the signs to establish if, indeed, my son could be manifesting any of them. I heard of and attended the 2017 Guaranty Trust Bank (GTB) Autism conference at Muson Center Lagos, Nigeria. The conference was part of the bank's corporate social responsibility. It was an annual initiative that aimed to give voice to the challenges faced by autistic individuals and provide practical assistance to enable them to function well as part of society. The conference attracted professionals from within and outside Nigeria who provide services to autistic individuals, such as behavioural specialists, occupational therapists, educators, caregivers, etc.

I remember telling some of my friends and family that I was attending the conference, and they were wondering what I was attending for. I didn't even know how to explain my intention, but I attended the conference anyway. The GTB Autism conference lasted for about three or so days, and from the first day, as I listened to speaker after speaker, I cried so much. I got emotional trying to decipher whether this autism label matched my son or not. As part of the conference activities, one of the days was reserved for parents or carers to take their children for assessment by a team of healthcare professionals, which included speech therapists, behavioural therapists, occupational therapists, etc. I took my son on the day we had pre-booked, and what a crowd of people attended. It was emotional to see children with varying needs and their parents or carers looking for support. Not much could be done with most children on that day. My son was recommended for further assessment at Lagos University Teaching Hospital (LUTH). We were to be seen by a psychiatrist. In Nigeria, psychiatrists carry out autism assessments and diagnoses. I was so exhausted after that day and worried for my son, thinking, will I ever get answers? There were so many children with severe needs on that day, and my heart wept, but my focus was on my son.

After the conference, I felt I was at least armed with information, and my major lesson learnt was the benefit of early intervention. My son's speech delay was a major known autism sign I could not over-look, but at least now I could make sense of what could be a probable cause. I told myself if I was not going to accept this autism label for my son, I could at least stop crying and take action now that he was still relatively young.

| 2 |

The Discovery (from age 2-3)

As my son approached his third birthday, we kept bombarding him with nursery rhymes and educational materials to improve his speech. I learnt about the importance of Docosahexaenoic acid (DHA) to brain development, and I knew speaking ability came from the brain. Therefore, I started a routine with my son, taking fish oil with high levels of DHA and other food supplements to support brain development.

At this time, he was now attending Home Science Nursery and Primary School in Lagos, Nigeria. We changed his school for many reasons, including the need to expose him to a larger class in the hope that exposure to more children would motivate him to speak. I remember his first week at the new school. I met his teacher to confirm how he coped with school. She said my son did not give her any trouble. She also said she noticed that he is a special child who does not learn things like others. She continued that they were helping him to hold his utensils correctly, play with other children better, respond to instructions by prompting, etc. Her counsel to me was never to compare my child to others. She said to give him time so we could discuss his progress further by the end of the term. If only this woman knew how much I wanted to hear those words. Finally, I had some positivity and hope outside of myself.

I resolved that if, by his third birthday, there was no major improvement in his speech, then we would consider speech therapy. While I knew he could benefit from other interventions like behavioural therapy, my primary focus was his speech. When upset, my son would throw himself on the floor, but thankfully, he never hit others, so I felt we could manage his behaviour. I researched and knew speech therapy was expensive, but I had to have a plan for my sanity's sake. I had soaked myself with so much information about autism and the strategies used to support it. I shared some of this information with my husband. I felt my husband was still trying to make sense of our reality, so I didn't bother him too much with my concerns anymore. I just went ahead and did what I felt needed to be done and then gave my husband feedback. Each day, I silently hoped and prayed that a miracle would happen. My son became my case study to determine if, indeed, there is any trace of autism. I saw autism at this time as something people had, like a disease.

One day, I asked my husband to take our son to Lagos University Teaching Hospital (LUTH) in Lagos, Nigeria for the psychiatric assessment recommended at the autism conference I had attended earlier. Overall, my interpretation of the outcome of that assessment was a mixed signal that suggested a wait-and-see approach. There was no formal autism diagnosis, but even if there had been, I wasn't ready to accept it. There was something in me that detested the idea of labels. I told myself my son was such a fine boy and a sweetheart, but the thought that anything could be wrong with him kept plaguing me. He had frequent meltdowns due to his inability to express himself. He was also fussy about eating and ate a few selected foods like golden morn cereal and jollof rice. He had minimal social interaction with peers, but those did not bother me as much as the speech delay.

My son was also having challenges with potty training; he just could not get it. His nanny was tasked to work with us on this specifically, and we would take him to the toilet several times a day for over a year. Sometimes, he would use the toilet, but other times, he would not. It was so difficult, and I often felt very frustrated. He also hated brushing his teeth, but we kept at it daily, trying to get him to learn these skills. From school and at home, we realised that he didn't like colouring, but with persistence, he did it sometimes. I was beginning to realise that my son sought to please me and those around him. I then decided to use this to motivate him to learn new skills. This worked sometimes with some activities like colouring.

My son was still very active; he just would not sit still. Going out with my son was a lot of work, as he would jump everywhere. I think he loves having open space to run around; he just wanted to be free. Some environments understood the need for young children to be free to run around, and some didn't. Nevertheless, I carried him everywhere I could where children could go. I thought to myself, in the worst-case scenario, when it became too much for him, and we had to chase him around, we would leave. I learnt early on not to cage him at home but to expose him to different experiences. At home, we talked to him and treated him like a human being, whether he responded to us or not.

I tried reading books to him to get him to learn to read, but he found it boring. So, I decided to use the tablet computer to read to him sometimes. We realised if the reading material had musical content, he would be fixated; otherwise, it was a no or, at best, minimal attention till he switched. However, my son won't sit still with the tablet computer; he runs all over the place, so there is no way of knowing whether he is learning. Regarding discipline, we lived in Nigeria, so spanking a child was not prohibited. We said, let us try spanking to see if it will help my son cooperate with all our efforts to get him to learn new skills. I was so fixated on him sitting calmly to learn as I was used to, and it frustrated me when I felt I was unsuccessful. I learnt much later that spanking him was counterproductive as it only made him anxious. I realised that my son has a solid retentive memory. In his way, he sang, i.e., made sounds along to the nursery rhymes, which he watched repeatedly. He still loved the alphabet and numbers and was always reciting them. He also learnt to identify body parts from the tablet computer, which meant he was reading from the tablet computer after all. I did not make the connection until later that he was learning independently.

We noticed after some time that my son was beginning to comprehend better and understood simple instructions like "Drop your plate", "Don't do that", etc. For instance, he would agree to drop his empty dirty plate in the kitchen but won't touch it if it is stained around the edges. He loved throwing objects up, anything with light, anything that spins, and closing doors were his favourite activities. He showed his excitement by jumping, running around, smiling, and making sounds. He was fascinated by people's faces, particularly people's noses and eyelashes. He would touch them with curiosity, and I just never understood why.

I have a friend called Lace, and one day, she asked me to pick up her colleague, Mrs Pink, who lived close to us. She and I talked, and she shared her son's story about learning to speak at three years and seven months. My son was not that age yet, but as she shared the story, I knew this was to encourage me that my son, too, would speak. She recommended her son's speech therapist to me. On the 11th of Oct 2017, the therapist started working with my son at school a few times a week. This was before he turned three years old. She used all sorts of unimaginable resources to work with him. She requested family photos to teach him; she asked us to buy alphabets, numbers, and common word charts. She also asked us to get a sensory brush she used on him in school. We started to see steady improvement in my son's independence around his third birthday. We were having success in his potty training many months after his third birthday. Some of the things we did was to create a toilet schedule in the morning when he woke up, after meals, and before bed. I think our consistency helped him eventually understand what was expected. The major lesson from this stage was hope. I didn't cry as much anymore. I was now more confident about staying on this course and ensuring the progress we were seeing in my son continued.

| 3 |

It was happening (from age 3-6)

We continued the sessions with the speech therapist, who was such a kind woman. She prayed for my son regularly, encouraged me, and shared strategies with me on what to do at home to complement her sessions with him at school. My son was beginning to gain speech and use language well into his third year, which was months after he started speech therapy. Oh, what a joy! He could now call me mummy with enough clarity that I could hear it. He improved at grasping new words and communicating his needs with one word. This progress renewed my hope and resolve. At this point, I knew there was no going back. We, too, at home, started working on him saying sentences, and he responded well by mimicking us. We also worked on speech clarity through repetition. He would say a word, and then we would repeat it so he would hear the right way to say it. I think he was also excited to hear his voice as he was so happy, maybe because we praised him a lot when he used his words.

At school, he was thriving; he was learning to write letters and numbers. He now knew his first name; he could tell us he was three years old. This was largely scripted language as his speech therapist shared the prompts she uses, but to me, it was progress. He was now beginning to tell us what he wanted to eat. At this stage, my son had a brother, and he was quite fond of his brother. He was always available to run errands like bringing his brother's things, giving him kisses, and generally playing with him. We were certainly not done teaching him. We progressed to teaching him how to have phone conversations and proper responses to conversations. Yes and No responses to conversations were still an issue, as he would repeat the questions after you instead. However, my son was getting better at mixing with his peers now. He's not just playing alongside them but actively with them sometimes. We're not sure whether having a brother contributed to this progress, but we were elated with any progress.

At almost four years, i.e., three years and ten months, to be precise, my son was reading books slowly, and the clarity of speech was also improving. He also used multiple words like phrases instead of just one word to request things. His dad, his nanny, and I just started working more on his independence at this point. I knew now he could hear, understand, and respond to us. We first taught him how to dress himself in shirts without buttons and trousers. His determination to learn was so evident at this stage, and I certainly used it to our advantage. His main strength was memorising and writing words. He also mastered 1-100 (in tens) without my help, and the tablet computer was a valuable tool for learning these things independently.

Also, he was doing better at sitting at a table and chair to eat, colour, and scribble with a pencil. He was eating well by himself, but we occasionally needed to prompt him to finish as he would be distracted and just sit there or try to do other things. This was such an improvement to earlier years. He still loved his tablet computer, and we carried it out to most places as it helped keep him calm and regulated. I was more successful at teaching him. He had homework from school in colouring, writing, etc., which I did with him. This stage was marked by remarkable growth in my son. My son could now answer yes and no questions, but he mixed them up sometimes. He knew how to say "help me," but he often had some episodes of frustration if we didn't respond quickly. My son was terrified of things like cleaning his ears with cotton buds or cutting his nails. He would scream, but we did it when needed anyway; compared to earlier years, cutting his hair at the barber's was now stress-free, and he sat calmly. Much kudos to his barbers at a small store located in Dolphin Estate, Ikoyi, Lagos, Nigeria for being so patient with him. Going out to parties and events still required him to be closely monitored, as he wouldn't sit still because of excitement. It can be overwhelming following him around as he wants to have his way, which can disrupt other people's fun. We worked on this for a long time, and it helped that he could now understand instructions. I had a way of changing the pitch of my voice or looking at him sternly, and my son understood that meant I was serious. My husband had his way, too, which was to be firm without raising his voice much, and my son understood not to cross certain boundaries. For instance, my son learnt to be careful with his tablet computer as he used to throw it up, and his Dad had to replace the screen so many times. My son just kept learning, including doing small chores like tidying up toys.

Well into his fourth year, my son learnt to say hello and bye to visitors to our house, but sometimes we have to prompt him. His speech clarity was so much better, and his confidence in speaking was now there. Going out with him at this stage was now less stressful as he listened and composed himself better. He could also tolerate staying in queues for a longer period compared to earlier years when he was restless and would try to run away or cry to be carried. I could also leave him in the children's church, for instance, at least for a few hours on Sundays. But he and his brother used to get into it, though, as sharing his tablet computer was a no-no.

In school, too, my son was doing so well he could add and subtract. He could recite both two and three-times tables from memory. It was clear from this stage that Maths would be his favourite subject. My husband said it was because Maths was logical, unlike other subjects. It felt like it was a progress explosion as he hit the five-year mark. Just before my son's fifth birthday, we stopped speech therapy as my son had improved in speech clarity and understanding. All the other elements of grammar, like tenses and proper sentence construction, were still in progress. I wish we could continue the therapy, but we just could not afford it anymore. My son was going to the toilet alone, though we still woke him up some nights and took him to the toilet. He didn't like sleeping alone, and brushing his teeth was still a struggle. However, he was no longer a fussy eater as he ate most foods in decent or little portions, depending on how familiar they looked. He also smelled his food before eating for reasons best known to him.

Looking back, I can say my son had a solid support system in Lagos, Nigeria. His teachers in school loved him, and every nanny he had at home loved him. Everyone who knew him loved him, including my sister, who doted on him so much. Don't even get me started about my Mum, who cooked his favourite jollof rice each week and brought it to us in large quantities as everyone in my house ate out of it. Aunty Lunar was on the school bus and did more than watch my son on the bus. In many ways, she was like his one-on-one support in school. The teachers knew to call her to get him to do his schoolwork. His default is to want to run around in school, which I understand they let him do sometimes, but he still managed to do schoolwork.

My son's vocabulary exploded from age six onwards, and he was now making full sentences. We could now have a conversation. However, some responses were scripted based on how he was taught by his therapist. This was a very fulfilling stage; all the prior challenges paled to insignificance compared to the progress. There was no perfection, though, as he would sit still for a short time when he had activities and run off after. He was still obsessed with closing doors he met open, and yes, he was afraid of pigeons. However, the best thing was my son could now sleep by himself. Some nights, though, he will wake up and join me and his Dad in our room. The lesson at this stage was that the desires my husband and I had regarding our son's development were now coming to pass. Not at all by the pace we wanted, but there was so much progress. I resolved to stay consistent with what we were doing as it was working.

| 4 |

The Transition (from age 7-8)

My husband and I had great plans for our family but felt somewhat limited in resources at our present location. We initiated a relocation plan, and our country of choice was the United Kingdom (UK). My motivation, as always, was to ensure my son had the best possible experiences in life.

I must confess I don't think we planned certain parts of the relocation in great detail. I was so fixated on the move and getting everyone settled in that I didn't think to prepare my son and my family for the intended move. I came to the UK months before the rest of my family, so finding a school place for my son was my responsibility. One mistake I made was not informing the school of the type of support my son needed. We did not have any formal diagnosis, so how was I to explain the support he needed? I took it for granted that many changes were happening simultaneously; for instance, the world was recovering from COVID-19, and I had just pulled my son out of his comfort zone, i.e., his solid support system in Lagos, Nigeria. I thought the new school would figure it out just like his old school did. That was a wrong move in retrospect. My fixation on not using labels on my son made me forget that we were in a new environment that recognised labels. I focused on intervention in Nigeria, and the system supported it as long as you could pay for the services. However, in the

UK, things were different. I was reminded that though my son was entitled to a school place to get adequate support to meet his needs, I had to notify the school that he was not a typical child. There was no figuring it out here; you must accept a label before being entitled to certain services. This was my interpretation of our new environment.

I was so excited that my son got a mainstream school place with ease at a primary school in Swansea, Wales. Based on his age at the time, he was placed in Year 2. My son struggled from the first day; hence, my excitement was short-lived. I got calls from his school about him throwing himself on the floor, crying, touching doors, not following instructions, or even using his words. I was deflated; I thought this boy had passed this stage; what was happening? Now, I know the transition was not managed properly. I felt like an irresponsible mother who just threw my son into a difficult situation. I now had to work with the school. Firstly, they reduced his school hours from full-time to part-time. Their reason was they needed to have additional support to monitor him in school closely. The school started to educate me on what needed to be done to support my son's education. I had to begin researching extensively to understand what this new environment we have moved to could offer my son. I knew I was at the mercy of the school at this stage, as I was entirely clueless. The school did a good job of keeping me informed and explaining things to me. I, in turn, took the time to explain each phase to my husband, as we both were responsible for my son. The school, without mincing words but with our consent, referred my son for an autism diagnosis assessment, which had a very long process. I could only fill out the questionnaire provided and submit it to the school, which then filled out their portion. Nothing much happened after we submitted the autism assessment all through our time in Swansea. Plus, COVID-19 restrictions were still ongoing, which meant a severe backlog. However, the school also informed me that it could take many years to have a formal autism diagnosis in Wales.

I told myself my family could not stay here if it would take such a long time for an assessment. I started researching and discovered we stood a better chance in England than in Wales. I started to pray for a plan to move to England as I felt access to resources was better there. We were in Swansea for a year, and my son struggled for the better part of it. He started to settle in, understand the new routines, etc, in the final term of our time in Swansea. The school hired a temporary staff member as one-on-one support for him, which helped him transition to full-time hours before we moved from Swansea. The son I knew back in Nigeria was returning and making progress. He could now use Yes and No correctly. His social skills improved greatly; he even said hello to strangers when we went out. He also started to follow instructions so well, with some objections at times.

An opportunity presented itself for my family to move to Cambridge, England, and I jumped on it. I informed my son's teacher and school head of our decision to move, and I felt they looked at me as an irresponsible mother. Who will move their child when he is finally beginning to settle down? Well, I did. I did so this time with a plan and knowledge. I took my time when I was researching school options to identify mainstream schools that prioritised inclusion and were committed to ensuring all children were supported in education. We secured a school place for my son in Year 3, and this time, I provided the school with all the information required to support him. I also ensured I prepared my son for this transition by telling him about his new school, class, teacher, etc. When my son resumed the new school, it took some time to settle in. At this stage, I knew my son's reliance on familiar routines. New routines took time for him to understand, but he coped better with time. His teacher and one-on-one support, which the school arranged, did their best to support him. A combination of continued positive reinforcement and the use of social stories helped my son learn the acceptable way to do things. For instance, learning to give people space as he still loved to hug and touch people's faces, which could be seen as inappropriate amongst his peers. My son's one-on-one gave me daily feedback on his performance. I, in turn, shared strategies that I knew could support him from our experiences at home.

Not too long after my son resumed at his new school, I was shocked to learn from the school's Inclusion Lead that we had to start the autism diagnosis assessment all over again, as Wales and England had different systems. The process for this was to take some time, but I was not too bothered about waiting anymore. My son's old school sent information to his new school, so the transition was better this time around. I was also informed about the process of getting an Education, health, and care plan (EHCP). This was another long process of completing forms, being assessed by psychologists, etc. Another round of research began because this was the first time I heard about EHCP. The school initiated the EHCP process, and we jointly provided the information on the forms and reviewed them before submitting them. It took some months to have the draft EHCP released, which set out my son's targets and the level of support to be provided. A short while after we accepted the draft, a final one was released. This EHCP was to serve as the blueprint for my son's education. The structure of the EHCP included learning outcomes sought with strategies to support them, timescale per learning outcome, and date of review. The key strategies to support my son largely included providing one-on-one support, timed learning to promote focus, and targeted support to improve social interaction. The EHCP is to be reviewed at certain intervals with the school to ensure my son was set the right targets and adequate support was provided. My son's targets were largely around behaviour, following instructions, communicating his needs, building familiarity with trusted adults, and other learning goals leveraging his strengths. I didn't leave all the work to the school as they did whatever they did in school; we also worked on the targets set at home.

We also started to think of extra-curricular activities as education is supposed to be a well-rounded endeavour. Our transition to the UK system made it clear that my son needed structure as he could easily get distracted. As one of his EHCP targets was improved focus, I researched activities that could help. I stumbled on music therapy with piano lessons and thought my son loved music, so why not? My husband also thought this was a good idea, so we committed to it. Through an online portal called Superprof, I found a piano teacher who was also a music therapist. What a woman! Neon made my son fall in love with the piano. She visited our house weekly for about an hour to teach my son. She was so good with him, very patient, talked to him calmly, and helped his confidence through constant encouragement. We started with a basic keyboard with few keys and then later advanced to a 61-key piano. My son learnt to play so well. The most remarkable thing was he would play a song a few times using the musical notes in sight and, after a while, would play from his memory. I could not believe it. The piano helped my son regulate, and he played every morning. I was pleased my son found an outlet to relax, improve his focus, and learn a new skill. The piano lessons were paid for, which came with sacrifices from my family, and Neon. She had a unique way of teaching; her commitment to my son was beyond what we could ever pay her for. I did not stop there; I also enrolled my son in group swimming lessons, which he went to weekly. A group called Little Fishes has well-trained teachers who are so patient with children of all abilities. It took a while, but after about 12 months, my son was swimming without float for short distances.

I also worked with my son at home to ensure his academic performance was improving. I realised the UK system, at least in primary school, did not challenge the children like that of Nigeria. For instance, I do not recall my son taking assessments for a while, and he was going to move to the next class either way. He was initially excluded from the assessments, and maybe the teacher thought he could not cope. I had to tell the teacher to allow him to take the assessments.

I knew if I wanted to get my son to learn to the standard I was used to, I had to support him at home. I did this for a while, getting Maths, English, reading books, etc, for his year group so we could learn at home. I didn't think his once-a-week school homework was sufficient for home learning. I wanted more, so I enrolled him in extra Maths and English classes from Year 4. I learnt about Tecnis, which was an online after-school program. The proprietress had Nigerian heritage, so I felt she would better understand the teaching standards I was used to. Tecnis is based on the UK curriculum, but as they prepared primary school children for the 11 Plus exam as well, I felt it would provide the right level of challenge I wanted for my son. My son learnt so much from this program, and his confidence improved. After a few months, he could do most of his homework; he started the program independently and always looked forward to his classes. He was now doing assessments in school consistently, and I was so happy with this. I told the teachers my son was taking paid extra classes, hoping they would no longer be reluctant to challenge him in school.

In Nigeria, I was so focused on my son that I did not realise that there were children and families around me who were having similar experiences. This was more glaring in the UK for reasons I can't explain. Could it be that I was now more aware or worrying less about my son? I learnt about neurodiversity, which changed my view of autism being a disease or something you had to a neurological condition. I also embraced the notion of autism being a spectrum. Still, I wouldn't say I like the autism label. I told myself if I were to accept any label for my son, it would be neurodivergent and on the spectrum. Both mean uniqueness to me and do not sound like a defect like autism does to me. Neurodivergent allowed me to acknowledge that my son's Creator, in His supremacy, allowed my son's brain to function in a way I could not understand, but it was not defective. Likewise, being on a spectrum suggests to me a spectrum of possibility and ability and, therefore, not something to be ashamed of.

The autism diagnosis report was released in 2023, which was about two years after we started the process. It was a lengthy process, and I believe we got to this stage because I opted for a remote assessment via Teams to fast-track it somewhat. My son was also assessed for Attention deficit hyperactivity disorder (ADHD), but that came out inconclusive. The report stated that the lack of focus my son exhibited in certain situations was linked more to autism. I have not shared the autism diagnosis report with my son, and I am in no rush to do so. The lesson at this stage is one of true acceptance of my son's uniqueness. This stage was one of growth and learning for my son and family. We made some mistakes earlier on, but we learnt from them. I remain determined not to limit my son by the label the world has placed on him. I have resolved that the label is to help the world make sense of his uniqueness. All I see when I look at my son is a champion, and I will never stop seeing him as anything less.

| 5 |

The Present (from age 9 to just before 10)

My son is still thriving in his academic and non-academic pursuits. He continued all the activities he started when he was about seven years old. My son now does piano lessons in school as Neon moved far away. In school, he plays an 88-key piano and he loves it. He is also still taking swimming lessons, as I want him to be a fully confident swimmer. My son's present interest is learning the meaning of words. He always comes to me asking what a new word means. I answer most of the time, and sometimes I throw it back to him to tell me; he knows the meaning most of the time. I have also taught him to use Google to learn the meaning of words.

He went through a phase where I don't know if he memorised the calendar or something. You tell him a date, and he will tell you what day of the week it was. This was remarkable; I just cannot understand how he does it. Another thing is his obsession with keeping to time. The worst thing you can ever do is to tell my son we are going somewhere at a particular time and not get there at that time. Being late really bothers him, and I don't know why. He thrives on routines at home and school, so we honour his schedules.

He is coping well in school and is presently in Year 5. At one point, I wished I could take him back a year and get him to repeat Year 4, for instance. You cannot do that in the UK public school system. I am now glad we did not have such options, as it was the motivation I needed to identify ways to support my son at his level. I am no longer obsessed with him catching up, and I have taken the time to understand the right pace he can work with. The right pace is a combination of challenging him but not going overboard. His present one-on-one in school is so lovely. She made me realise that my son's eyes needed to be checked as he always wanted to sit close to the board. She was right; we had to get my son glasses as we learnt he was short-sighted. We work together so well, and she tells me about my son's day. If I left this to my son only, he would leave out many details, especially the ones where his name goes on the log for making wrong choices they call them. I have learnt to take such reports as part of his learning and use them as opportunities to identify what he could have done better. He often promises his Dad and me that he will be on his best behaviour before he leaves for school. He still likes to please and gets very emotional if he feels he has let us down. His performance in school is good enough for me as I know he is doing his very best. His favourite subject is Maths. He excels in arithmetic, but math word problems need to be broken down and explained step by step before he gets it. He reads at least a book each school day, and this has helped his comprehension not only in English but in other subjects as well. He is reading at the right level for his age, but his comprehension is not yet at the same level. The best thing is he loves school and learning, and this can only mean improvement in my eyes.

He still plays with his tablet computer, but he uses it now more to play games and watch YouTube. His YouTube content is filled with songs, learning facts, some cartoons, etc. His Dad and I look for opportunities to turn his interest in the tablet computer into another learning adventure. We recently enrolled him in a computer coding program. We opted for a physical class as I am focused on building his social skills. My son tells me he has friends in school, and most of them are girls. I imagine girls tend to be kind, which resonates well with him. But more recently, I have been hearing some boy names, too. We keep encouraging him to try in this area, and it's great that there is some progress. I cannot adequately tell if my son's peers, especially at school, perceive him as different, as he does keep to himself a lot of times. I am told his classmates are generally kind to him, but I am mindful that he has his one-on-one with him most times. We have taught him to be bold to tell an adult if anyone treats him in an unkind manner, as he knows how to speak up for himself. I just want him to have real buddies, but to be fair, he is quite fond of his cousin Kite, so I know he can make friends. Friendship takes time, so we are on a journey and will get there.

At home, my son is very independent. He prepares each day, including wearing clothes with buttons and laces. We must remind him to look in the mirror to ensure everything is in place. His default response is to rush self-care activities or anything he sees as a chore. I make his meals or pack his school lunch, ensuring nothing is left out. I allow him to eat school food sometimes to interact with peers and explore other cuisines. He takes him and his brother to bed each night by 8 pm except maybe on school holidays without prompting. I am so proud of him, as we have come such a long way. We keep teaching him skills for independence, like cleaning the dishes, vacuuming, and brushing some areas. We will keep at it, as his independence is something I have always been committed to. The lesson at this stage is one of truly living. I was fixated for too long on what my son could not do, but that has all changed. My focus now and beyond is my son's strengths. We will hone his skills and make him great at everything he is good at.

Looking Ahead: My concluding letter to my son

My dear son,

I started by reminding you of who you were. You are "a champion". I will now end by reminding you of what you do so well. Don't be too concerned about what you cannot do yet; remember all you achieved on your way to 10 years.

1. You play the piano beautifully, love music, and have specific tunes you listen to daily.
2. You love your brother, but you no longer take nonsense from him, so you can speak up and stand up for yourself in any situation.
3. You are very kind and loving and still give loads of hugs and kisses.
4. You eat almost everything now; oh my goodness, you eat a lot now. You can make some of your meals independently, like making a sandwich and warming your food in the microwave.
5. You can ride a bicycle, and you recently told me that once you turn ten, you'll start riding on your own, even to the shops.
6. You are learning new languages like Yoruba, Spanish, and French.
7. You have told me bouncing around with your rope is important to you, so I let you stim away without interfering too much.
8. You told me you want to become a police officer. You have my support whether or not this changes.

9. You like going out to play areas, parties, events, parks, etc, but for a short while as you prefer to be home in your own space.

10. You become highly motivated when praised, and you do a great job of praising yourself after completing something that initially seemed difficult.

I love that you can now tell me exactly what you want, like you want a party for your 10th birthday, and you will have the party, I promise. I am thrilled when you tell me I look good on the days I dress up. I love that you always ask how I am feeling. You also tell me you love me many times daily, making me very happy. You, my dear son, have beat the odds; I have pushed you, and so did your Dad; oh, we pushed, but you did not disappoint us. I am so proud of your accomplishments and encourage you to stay committed to your development. The greatest gift I could ever give to you, my dear son, alongside education, is for you to know God. I hope that you do grow to know God for yourself, as knowing God makes life worth living.

You are about to enter a wonderful season in your life, and I am no longer afraid. I look forward to your continued independence as you write your story from here henceforth. I know the journey ahead is beautiful as you continue to thrive beyond the label.

Yours truly,

Mummy

A letter to parents and carers

Dear Parent/ Carer,

I commend your dedication to supporting your child. While every child is unique, I want to share some key insights from my experiences that might be useful.

One important area is the benefit of early intervention. The emotional roller coaster you may experience is entirely valid, but it's crucial to take action once you notice your child lagging behind developmental milestones. Milestone charts can serve as a helpful guide, though they are not meant for direct comparison. Once you have established that your child is way behind in any milestone, identify ways to support that child. Trust your instincts; if you sense something is out of place in your child's development, do not ignore it. Observe, articulate it, and ask for help as soon as possible. Prioritise taking action now, even if your child is no longer young. Whether or not you choose to get a diagnosis, there must be a set of actions you are consistently carrying out to support your child's development. Even more so, a diagnosis process takes time, so use the waiting period to support your child in the best possible way. You will know when something is not right, even if others may tell you otherwise.

A critical one is the importance of constantly observing your child. It would help if you study your child continually. For instance, what they like or don't like, how they act in specific situations, what triggers certain behaviours, etc. Apart from observing your child, you need to familiarise yourself with the resources and services available to you and your child. Learning and relearning are constant on the journey to supporting your child's development, as strategies that work at certain stages might need to be adapted or even changed as the child grows. Understanding your child and having some information about the services supporting your child will likely position you for success as you seek further professional help if required.

Another is the value of seeking professional opinion and contribution. Professionals trained to support children, like doctors, educators, therapists, and others, add value to your efforts. Engaging their expertise when necessary helps identify proven resources and strategies to support your child. Asking for and receiving help is not a sign of failure but strength. You might be tempted to think you know your child best. This might be true in some sense, but it should not be a deterrent to receiving help from professionals. Scrutinise the information received from these professionals and apply them. Evaluate their effect on your child over a period to determine suitability. You are the voice of that child till they can advocate for themselves. Use that voice to access resources your child is entitled to from the community, school, and healthcare services. Don't keep silent when resources or services your child is entitled to are delayed or not granted. Be relentless in your pursuit of getting the help your child requires at any cost.

Don't be in a hurry to teach too many skills simultaneously. It helps to focus on a few skills to increase the chance of success. Once the child has mastered the one or two skills you are working on over time, you move to the next one. This does not mean you should not challenge the child. Challenge the child within realistic limits, focusing on what your child can accomplish over a certain period. Always have your child's needs in mind, not your desires or aspirations, when setting goals for the child to achieve. Don't compare your child's pace with other children. Identify your child's learning style and use this to teach new skills, even if the child's learning style might look unconventional or unpopular.

The school and health systems can do their best to support your child, but the most impactful learning happens at home. The home is largely your child's safe place, so use this to your advantage. Be committed to supporting learning at home if possible and involve everyone in the home to support the learning for consistency in your absence. Be creative and make learning fun to encourage the child, especially if they are very young. Setting goals and having a plan for each developmental stage is useful. But be prepared to adapt the plan to suit your child and the progress made over time. Don't forget to recognise that it might take time for your child to learn something new. Your task is to stay motivated and committed to your child's development. Be intentional about the child's development and do not relent, especially when you have ascertained that the child has the potential to learn the skill. Identifying and leveraging your child's strengths is the key to recognising the child's potential. It also potentially ensures the child will cooperate with your efforts.

We live in exciting times with the proliferation of technology and smart devices. I encourage you to use these to your advantage. Tablets and Augmentative and alternative communication (AAC) applications and devices have been proven to support the development of communication. See these devices as tools to complement other strategies you are engaged in. Opinions on relying on technology may vary, but the priority is whether it supports your child's development. Do all you can to implement safety controls for your child if you choose to adopt any of these tools. I encourage you to embrace any and every tool, if possible, if it supports your child's development.

Be mindful to celebrate every progress made in your child's development. Do not just celebrate it; share each step with professionals and non-professionals, like family and friends working with you to support your child. Remember that your child's win is a win for you as well. Share the progress and strategies you used to achieve them so all those supporting your child can have adequate information.

Also, please do not ignore your needs; it's so easy to get burned out by the myriad of sacrifices you might have to make. Take time for your interests and live as it helps strengthen you for the journey ahead. Do not hide away, as your child's uniqueness is nothing to be ashamed of. Please do your best to surround yourself with people who inspire hope, as it helps clarify every course of action required to support your child. Be kind to yourself don't let anyone judge you wrongly or put you down for your decisions. Even if you make mistakes, learn from them and move on; you are wonderful and deserving of many applauses.

Finally, you need a support system to promote healthy emotional and mental well-being, amongst other reasons. The rest of this book will explain my family's experiences with my son attaining key milestones like reading, writing, potty training, riding a bicycle, and some self-care activities. I hope we can build a supportive community to uplift each other through our respective journeys. It will be a community focused on sharing, learning, and possibly easing the burden where possible as you work to support your child's development. I want you to know that you are seen, not alone, and someone out there is rooting for you.

Yours truly,
A fellow parent.

PART 2

Strategies to support learning new skills at home

| 6 |

Learning to read (from age 2-5)

Reading Readiness

I started teaching my son to read when he was about two years old. At that age, he was introduced to the alphabet and numbers through nursery rhymes and word-to-picture matching games on his tablet computer. I therefore thought we could convert this recognition ability into reading. I first started trying to read to him using picture books and short story books. I was not always successful, as he would not sit still to listen to me read to him. It would only last a few minutes on the days I managed to read to him.

Adapted Techniques

I was initially too focused on getting my son to sit beside me or across me from a table and chair to read. My son was too active for that, so I changed my strategy by installing age-appropriate reading applications on his tablet computer. I utilised his attachment to his tablet computer instead of sticking to just paper books. He responded better to his tablet computer and accessed the reading applications periodically. He often preferred to use it on his terms without anyone's guidance. I struggled to accept this initially, but I later realised he would sound out words as he watched his tablet computer. He was not speaking yet then, so it was more sounds he made. For over a year, I continued to find ways to get him interested in picture books by reading to him, even for a few minutes.

He learnt phonics songs from YouTube content he watched on his tablet computer between two and three years old. However, he didn't apply phonics successfully in how he sounded words even as he started to gain speech at three years old. I think he learnt words as whole words by sight and not breaking them down using phonics. For new words, when we tried to use phonics to teach him to pronounce, he didn't get it, so instead, we chose to say the words and let him echo back to us. This was how I started to leverage his retentive memory to support his reading and learning in general.

My son worked with a speech therapist between ages three and four who used flashcards as a communication tool. The therapist tried to follow the Picture Exchange Communication System (PECS) using the flashcards. However, my son chose to read out the words from these cards instead of using them for communication, so the flashcards were used more to support his reading.

Motivation

I recall we tried to attach rewards to get him to do many things, including reading, but this was not always successful. Instead, we realised that praising him on the days that he attempted to read independently or with our guidance was the right motivation. For instance, when he reads words from his tablet computer or even from watching the TV, we say "good job" and make a big deal of each attempt. I also corrected any errors immediately. If he mispronounced a word, I would model the right way to pronounce it, prompting him to say it after me, which he did sometimes.

Routine and gradual progression

My son started school before he turned two years old, so he had an established routine. As with most of the skills he developed, we used this familiarity with routines to our advantage. From about three to four years old, on school days, I incorporated reading in any form consistently as part of his after-school activities at home. His nanny or I would sit with him on the floor or a chair and encourage him to read. He began to recognise and read words as we pointed to them in the picture-based single-word books we used. After a while, we moved from picture books with words to picture books with short sentences.

We eventually moved to short text-only books after some time as well. The goal was to get him to read at least a few pages from each book correctly, without necessarily finishing it in one sitting. Over about one year, we progressed this way based on how correctly he was reading the books. We read the books over and over, which must have helped him. Similarly, on his tablet computer, with the reading applications, the goal was reading accuracy, not volume. From about four years old, as he gained more speech and understanding, we asked simple questions about the books as he read, like "What colour is the apple?" "What shape is the box?" etc. At this age, he knew abstract concepts like colours and shapes, and so we used that to support reading and a bit of comprehension. It was a gradual process of following his lead most of the time that worked.

On days when he was not keen to follow our reading schedule, we tried again another time but stayed consistent. With each stage of his development, we transitioned into appropriate levels of reading material till he learnt to read independently. The experiences shared cover my son's second to fifth year. Beyond his fifth year, he eventually saw reading as part of his school and after-school activities. Also, his homework from school consistently included reading in one form or another, so he had many opportunities to develop his reading ability.

| **7** |

Learning to write (from age 2-5)

Writing readiness

Conventional wisdom suggests that a child's readiness must be assessed before teaching new skills. I did not follow this when I decided to start teaching my son how to write. Like reading, I just went with it since he was already exposed to tracing alphabets and numbers with his finger using his tablet computer. We had installed many interactive kids' applications, including some writing ones, which he frequently used independently. We started teaching him how to write while we were teaching him to read. I would say because he started school before he turned two years old, I felt he had to learn these skills early. In retrospect, I don't think using this as a motivation for teaching him any skill, much less writing, was wise. The process might have been a little less tedious if I had considered conventional wisdom and started when he was ready.

At around two years, my son started to hold his utensils to feed himself, but his grip was still not strong enough. I wasn't concerned about his fine motor skills and thought that, with time, he would have a firmer grip on the utensils. We also introduced colouring activities to him, on and off, using colouring books with familiar items like fruits and animals, but he did not enjoy them. We switched between crayons and coloured pencils to promote interest in colouring activities. I thought he lacked interest in colouring because he disliked sitting still, but he probably was not ready. He was holding the crayons and coloured pencils correctly, unlike his utensils, but he just did not like colouring as an activity. I thought that since he could hold the crayons and coloured pencils correctly, this was enough of an ability to introduce writing. Despite all these unreadiness signs, I went ahead, and we started with plain pieces of paper and pencils. He struggled as I did not take the time to teach initial steps like proper grip and hand positioning before attempting to get him to write. I later realised that having plain pieces of paper and telling him to write the letter A, for instance, was not yielding results. I also tried to model how to write by holding his hands so we could do it together, but that did not help either. I decided to put a hold on it all for some time as I thought we were trying to teach him too many things simultaneously. However, he continued playing with his tablet computer's letter and number tracing applications.

Step-by-step process

My son was beginning to get writing activities from school between three and four years old, so this prompted me to start teaching him how to write again. For instance, as homework on some days, he brought back a letter or number tracing exercise from school for us to do and return to school. We already had all sorts of writing materials at home; some were given to us as gifts, and others we bought. They included dotted or lined tracing books containing uppercase and lowercase letters with numbers, pencils, sharpeners, and erasers. At this age, my son's ability to follow instructions had also improved, so I used it to our advantage. He was also holding his utensils correctly and more confidently at this stage. Plus, he could now tolerate sitting on a chair with a table for short periods, providing the right opportunity to teach him by sitting next to him.

His nanny and I worked together on teaching him how to write. We introduced the tripod grip using his right thumb, index, and middle fingers straightaway so we would not need to change the style later. He did not struggle too long to get the grip, but it took some time before his grip on the pencil appeared firm. I think he embraced this pencil grip due to exposure, as I suspect that is how they were teaching him in school. We asked him to scribble lines on pieces of paper using the correct pencil grip, which I think went on for months. We later introduced the tracing book, starting with the pages with lines to trace. There were dotted vertical, horizontal, curved, zig-zag lines to serve as the foundation before trying to trace letters or numbers. We allowed him to spend some time on lines, and as you might expect, he traced outside the dotted lines on some days, and on other days, he followed the dotted lines. We started prompting him by telling him to follow the lines. His grip on the pencil also improved at this stage, as what started as light strokes became more legible with time.

After tracing lines consistently, we introduced pages of the tracing book with dots forming different uppercase letters. Initially, we placed our hands over his to show him what was expected. As with writing lines, we prompted him to trace the dots to form the letter. He would follow the dots correctly in some instances, and in others, he would trace outside the dots. We just continued practising and correcting errors as a joint activity; his nanny or I did this with him. We later also started to mix things up by reintroducing blank paper. We encouraged him to draw lines on pieces of paper. We wanted to see how well he could write without following dots or lines. I think he found writing on paper more comfortable, as the lines or dots meant he had to focus more. It was more free-form on paper, so maybe that helped him relax more. To add an element of variety, we also gave my son a chalkboard and magnetic writing pad to practice writing. He liked these and must have seen this more as play, especially as he did not need to sit at a table with anyone, unlike writing with a pencil and book or paper. We were mixing things up at this stage, and these various options may have helped his pencil grip become firmer.

Tracing the dots for lowercase letters came next. We were just following the pattern of the book, and there was no particular reason for using uppercase letters before lowercase letters. But in retrospect, there must have been a reason the book was structured with lines first, followed by letters and numbers.

Repetition and Consistency

My son's tracing in books with dots and writing on plain paper continued beyond his third and fourth years. Writing became part of his after-school activities before or after reading. We just continued introducing various opportunities for him to write consistently, and the activities from school helped with this. For instance, he had writing exercises to complete and return to school. He was writing single letters and even numbers before he turned four.

At this stage, we were not concerned about the size of his writing, whether he was writing big or small. Neither were we concerned when he wrote outside the line in books with lines. We would praise his efforts if he wrote something that looked like a letter. Naturally, some letters were easier for him to write correctly compared to others. I cannot recall with certainty which letters were easier for him to write first, but it took some time before we could say he wrote all the letters legibly. Also, I cannot recall if he preferred to write in lowercase rather than uppercase, but I know he developed the ability to write both.

Continuous reinforcement

Writing words was the next logical step after my son learnt to write letters and numbers. We continued to use tracing books and plain sheets of paper as before. He first traced dotted words before copying whole letters to form words without dots. My goal was for him to develop the ability to write whole words, not necessarily joining the letters together. It was at this stage that I realised my son was writing slowly. I cannot remember his exact age, but it must have been before he was five years old, as he was becoming more conversational in his speaking abilities. I recall it took him time to complete such activities as he started writing anything longer than single letters. I was not too bothered about speed; I was just pleased he was writing. We encouraged him as he wrote and praised him by saying "good job" or giving "high fives" for his efforts.

From five years old onwards, writing words became writing phrases and then writing sentences, which we later incorporated with other learning activities. For instance, as he now knew how to spell his name at this stage, we would ask him to write his name, write how old he was, etc. As my son moved higher in class, there was an expectation from his school to focus on handwriting by emphasising the importance of joining letters, proper letter placement on lines, using upper and lower cases correctly in sentences, and adding punctuation marks. I was in no rush to teach my son these handwriting skills. His teachers may have focused more on handwriting in school because my son picked up these skills along the way. I used more of a correction tactic to encourage handwriting skills instead of the step-by-step process we initially used to teach him to write. For instance, if I spotted any error in his writing work, I used the opportunity to tell him to correct it. I had learnt not to put him under pressure anymore and to give him the freedom to figure out certain things independently. The goal was for him to learn to write, which he did accomplish.

| 8 |

Potty Training (from age 2-6)

Support system's readiness and commitment

I initially set a goal for my son to be potty trained before his third birthday, but that did not happen. It was an unrealistic goal as my family was still trying to understand how to effectively communicate with my son. We still started the process many months after his second birthday, as he had started school. We had a nanny at home who took care of him after school, so we decided to start teaching him at home. Everyone in my home had to be part of the process. Once it was clear that my husband, my son's nanny, and I were all committed to this, we decided to start. Our first task was to purchase a potty and pull-up diapers. Throughout the process, we shared information on what was working and what was not to ensure we followed the same plan.

Signs of readiness

The next step was to try to identify physical signs to indicate when my son was likely to need the toilet. For instance, we set out to identify the sign he was giving us that he needed the toilet, like taking off his diaper. This was difficult as we did not initially see any signs of readiness. We started anyway by taking him to the toilet and guiding him to sit on the potty. We sometimes took the potty from the toilet and brought it into the living room to get him to sit on it, but we had no success most of the time. He did not like sitting on the potty; we knew this because he usually showed no interest. We aimed to get him to sit on the potty for a while to encourage urinating there, at least. After a few weeks, we decided to eliminate the potty and take him to sit on the toilet seat directly. We did not have success with this either. He did not urinate in the toilet, as it was clear at the time my son had not made the connection or understood why he was being taken to the toilet at random times. We, therefore, decided to pause the potty-training activities for some time till we were sure he understood any instructions we were going to be giving. I was exhausted and almost gave up, but I knew we had to reevaluate and continue at another time.

Routine

My son had a clear routine, which I felt he had mastered over the six months or so period he had been going to school. For instance, when he woke up, he knew he would brush his teeth, bathe, have breakfast, wear school clothes, etc. We then decided to incorporate taking him to the toilet at specific times to help him connect with urinating. So, when he woke up, we took him to the toilet first. Minutes after each meal or drink, we took him to the toilet. Just before he left home for school, we took him to the toilet, and when he got back from school, we took him to the toilet and before bed. We did this all through age two and most days, we had no success, but we kept at it.

Communication

We were beginning to realise around my son's third birthday that he understood simple instructions and then decided this could be the time to intensify our ongoing potty training efforts. We started using keywords like "toilet time" to prompt him before or as we were taking him to the toilet to urinate. We had eliminated the potty and were putting him to sit directly on the toilet. We noticed that he at least knew what we were asking, as he would willingly follow our lead to the toilet. On most days, we had no success, but we kept at it because at least we felt he now knew the reason he was being taken to the toilet.

Holidays

I realised that having a consistent schedule alone was insufficient, so I decided to utilise one end-of-year school holiday, generally lasting six to seven weeks. This idea came from one of the multiple resources I researched to learn how to potty train my son. I then purchased regular cotton pants to supplement the pull-up diapers we had already started with. Most of the time we were at home, we would keep him in pants without trousers. We also increased the frequency of taking him to the toilet to about two to three hours apart from the initial schedule we had started, e.g., taking him to the toilet after meals. This still was not enough as most times, before we even took him to the toilet, he had urinated on himself. The only benefit was that it was more visible with the pants, so we could clean him up immediately. However, we used this time to teach him how to pull down and pull up his pants when we took him to the toilet. After the holiday, we returned to the diapers but periodically wore regular pants for him when we would be home all day.

Modelling

We decided to try to model to him how boys use the toilet. Remember that we had not even mastered identifying my son's physical signs for his readiness to use the toilet. But I still felt teaching him other things around potty training would support our objectives. So sometimes, when his dad went to the toilet, he took our son with him to stand by him to watch him. I, too, started making a big deal of going to the toilet. When I had his attention, I would sometimes announce, "Mummy is going to the toilet". We did this while maintaining a toilet schedule between ages two and three.

Adapted Techniques

As mentioned earlier, we abandoned the potty early on and focused more on putting my son directly to sit on the toilet. We also wanted to adopt techniques that could be used in any environment, like home, school, etc. I felt it would help with the various potty training steps later on. We continued sticking to the toileting schedule that we had developed, which incorporated the already established routines he was used to. For instance, he now knew that once he woke up, the next went to the toilet, and after eating, the next went to the toilet, etc. I think this was one of the things that helped my son. Following routines was already a part of his life, so perhaps it helped him make the connection. After almost a year of following the routine, my son was more consistently using the toilet each time we took him to urinate.

Positive reinforcement

My son loves to be praised, so we used this to our advantage. We used keywords like "good job" to praise him when he successfully used the toilet to urinate. I also could not hide my frustration at times he wet himself, for instance. I think he must have noticed this as well, as he liked it when anyone praised him. We noticed that over time, possibly about a year since we started seeing progress with urinating, my son started trying to take himself to the toilet. It was at this stage we started to pay more attention to any physical signs. We followed him when we saw him going to the toilet, stood by the door, watched him, and when he was done, we praised him loudly, even giving hugs sometimes, which he liked.

Prompting, incorporating physical signs

We kept noticing physical signs my son made when he wanted to use the toilet. The schedule was a great start, but it was not enough. For instance, we noticed he would stand still and sometimes progress toward the toilet. When he went into the toilet, on some occasions, he would just stand still, but after a while, when he checked his diaper, it was wet. He also had a particular spot where he went to stand when he wanted to pass a stool. Our initial focus was to notice the signs for when he wanted to urinate, but then we also observed the signs for when he wanted to pass a stool. This was a major turning point, so when he indicated any of the signs, we would prompt him by asking, "Toilet time?" His response will be either that he walks toward the toilet to indicate yes or not respond, which we interpreted as no. We continued this for many months till we established a clear pattern.

Visual guides

My son learns a lot from his tablet computer, so we incorporated potty training videos with a musical element to gain his attention. We identified a few videos from YouTube we played regularly. A combination of the consistent schedule and the videos may have helped.

Gradual process

As previously mentioned, within the first year, our focus was to master the urinating phase so that he consistently urinated in the toilet. Along the way, he picked up knowing how to take his pants off, put the pants back on, and then wash his hands, as this was added to the toilet routine. Now, as his understanding grew and as we had better knowledge of the physical signs, we added the gradual elimination of diapers, first during the day and then much later at night. At some point, we added flushing and teaching the distinction between standing to urinate and sitting to pass a stool. It was very fulfilling to see him eventually learn to stand to urinate in the toilet instead of sitting.

Teaching my son to wipe after using the toilet came last; after over two years, we started the potty training process. We tried to do things step by step, but in some cases, it felt like at a stage, after many unsuccessful tries, he mastered multiple steps simultaneously, so we went along with it.

Knowledge sharing and preparing for accidents

As we mastered my son's toilet routine at home, we were ready to share our experience with the school to support him as well. This started around his fourth birthday. But we still wore him pull-up diapers outside of the house till we were more confident. The more unused diapers we had from school, the more we knew we were progressing. We applied the same strategy on days we were going out, too. We adopted timed toilet breaks and wore pull-up diapers until he could go out without them. We always carried diapers and changes of clothes whenever we were outside the home as we could not rule out accidents.

Patience

The potty-training process took about three years before we got to confidently take my son outside the house without diapers. We also included wiping at a later stage. First, we did the wiping for him, then talked him through the process as we wiped him. Then we started giving him many chances to wipe himself as we watched, and then much later, he could wipe independently without guidance. I recall my son's potty-training journey being quite difficult, but we kept at it by adapting along the way.

My son's second and third year was a potty-training learning experience. We started by trying to understand the physical signs, adapting techniques, and establishing a means of communication. As we became successful in those, his third to fourth year was largely around consistently following routines and teaching independence. This was around when he started communicating his needs with one word and phrases, which helped our objectives.

All through my son's fourth and fifth years, it was a combination of consistently using established schedules, prompting him sometimes by following the physical signs he gave when he wanted to use the toilet. At this stage, he had learnt to speak, which helped a lot with his independence as he could now communicate to us when he needed to use the toilet. This was especially important when he was outside our home, i.e., in school. By his sixth year, he had achieved toilet independence as we had little or no accidents, including at night. However, we still supported my son with wiping after he used the toilet until we were certain it was no longer necessary.

| **9** |

Learning to ride a bicycle (age 7)

Built familiarity

From my son's one-year birthday, we had four-wheelers and tricycles at home given to him as gifts to play around with till about age five. He was more fascinated by spinning the wheels in his earlier years than anything else. We then started to redirect him from about three years old to see the tricycles as something he could sit on and ride instead of playing with as a toy. My son had no challenges with his gross motor skills, so we first focused on building his familiarity and confidence in sitting on the tricycle and four-wheelers. He would sit on them, and we would push him around in them. After a while, we didn't have to push him around in them. He learnt to move the tricycle and four-wheelers by placing his legs on the floor and moving backwards or forwards. He then learnt to put his legs on the pedals and turn the handles to turn the tricycle wheels. From around his fifth birthday, we decided it was time to teach him how to ride a bicycle. We got him a bicycle with training wheels, also called stabilisers.

Step-by-step process

After my son's fifth birthday, his nanny took the time over a long six-week holiday period to teach him how to first get on and off a bicycle, then how to sit on a bicycle and place his leg on the pedals, how to pedal when stationary, how to balance on a bicycle and eventually how to combine all the steps. She started indoors first to master the various steps, then moved outdoors with him to create more space. Getting my son to learn the steps took a whole long holiday. After the long holiday, his nanny continued to practice with him as they did over the holidays on some weekends or weekdays after school. This they did till he could cycle for short distances. I did not know how to ride a bicycle then, so his nanny taught him. He mastered riding a bicycle with training wheels when he was between five and six years old, and at the time, we lived in Lagos, Nigeria.

Modelling

We lived in the United Kingdom (UK) when my son was seven. My son had no nanny to teach him anymore, so it was left to me or my husband to teach him. We didn't prioritise this until we moved to Cambridge from Wales, where we realised young children cycled to school. This was the motivation I needed to learn to ride a bicycle. We first had to buy bicycles for my husband, me, and my son. I then set myself a target to learn to be better equipped to teach my son. I watched YouTube videos and learnt to ride a bicycle over many months. After learning to cycle, I felt ready to teach my son how to ride a bicycle without training wheels. As we approached summer, I decided to use this time to start to teach him by showing him how I rode the bicycle on multiple occasions. With no training wheels, the first task was teaching him how to balance on the bicycle.

Motivation

Throughout the weeks, I taught my son to ride a bicycle; I told him that learning this skill would mean we could ride to the park, for instance. I guessed he looked forward to the opportunity to ride the bicycle away from our house, which was where we were learning.

When I saw any child riding a bicycle during school drop-offs or pick-ups, I encouraged him to watch and motivated him by saying he could someday ride to school. I knew this would motivate him to keep up with our learning sessions at home.

Visual aids

The tablet computer was useful, as always, in teaching my son. I found a useful YouTube self-help video of children being taught to ride a bicycle without training wheels. Over the weeks I taught my son, I encouraged him to watch the videos before we went outside and continue learning to ride the bicycle.

Routine

As with most learning activities, we incorporated it with my son's after-school activities. Over a few weeks, at least three to four times a week, I took my son and his bicycle outside to an open space for him to learn. He learnt how to balance on the bicycle by me holding on to the bicycle seat as he pedalled for short distances. I gradually started to stop holding the bicycle seat for short periods and then longer periods till he got it. As usual, I praised his efforts continually and followed his lead. If he said he was tired, we went back inside the house and tried again another time without putting him under pressure. I was persistent, though, because he initially found it quite challenging, especially before he knew how to balance on the bicycle.

A combination of consistency and encouragement helped his confidence eventually. His confidence grew after learning to balance on the bicycle, and then I added other elements, like braking and turning at angles. We practised outside our home for many weeks before we attempted to go outside our neighbourhood.

Self-care activities (from age two onwards)

Self-Care readiness

I was committed to teaching my son self-care skills to support his independence at various stages of his development. I deliberately assessed my son's readiness before trying to teach him this set of skills. Any self-care skills he learnt at various stages of his development were tailored to his abilities at any given time. As with most of the skills he learnt at home, everyone was involved, including his nanny, me, and his dad. We had established a means of communicating with him from about three years old, so my anxiety about teaching him these skills was reduced. The steps we used are probably like how you would teach any child but with some adaptations, including modelling with patience.

One of the self-care activities my son learnt early was eating with utensils. We started this before he turned two years old. Before then, we sat across him as he sat on his little chair and table to feed him his meals. We purchased age-appropriate cups, cutlery, and waterproof toddler bibs and just started by taking it one day at a time. Firstly, it was how to drink from an open cup. Before turning two, he already knew how to drink from bottles with straws. We started using a plastic cup with a handle and placed it within my son's reach on a console table in our living room. My son spent most of his time in the living room when he was not in school. He was not yet speaking then, so we were advised to keep things he often requested out of reach to prompt him to ask for them. But for learning to drink from a cup purpose, we kept a cup of water within reach so he could see it and attempt to reach for it even if no one was available. We also placed a cup of water beside him at mealtimes to build familiarity. We ensured that the cup was only filled partially to reduce spills and make it easy for him to lift to drink. He had many opportunities to practice with our guidance. I do not recall it taking a long time before he learnt to drink from an open cup, but as with many things, he did things slowly at first, and later, the speed picked up as he became confident.

At age two, my son ate only a few meals, like cereal and rice, so we first started with a spoon. As you would expect, at the beginning, we had to wear the bibs at mealtime so he would not stain his clothes as food dropped. Thankfully, he did not resist wearing the bibs and had one for school. He was not speaking then, so we just modelled to him how to use the spoon. He held the spoon close to the tip for a very long time, and even when we tried to correct him, we noticed that was his preference. He also took his time eating, as it took many seconds for him to scoop the food with the spoon and put it in his mouth. We held ourselves back from rushing him and just allowed him to learn at his pace. At school, they also helped to teach him how to hold the spoon correctly as he sat to eat with his peers at mealtimes. Eventually, my son learnt to hold the spoon closer to the middle, which helped reduce food dropping as he scooped it. As his grip became firmer, we eliminated the bib. Also, as he started to eat different varieties of foods beyond age three that required picking, we introduced a fork. Chunky food like chips is what we started him with using a fork. Using the fork independently was an easier transition compared to using the spoon. We modelled it a few times, and he got it. He still ate slowly, using either a fork or spoon for many years, and I cannot recall at what age his eating speed became as you would expect.

Cutting food came in many years later, possibly from age eight, till I was sure I could trust him with a knife. I was not worried about motor skills; I think it was more cautious and convenient than ability or readiness when I introduced a knife to him. I am unsure if he used cutlery sets in school as he ate in the school canteen from age seven when we moved to the UK. In Lagos, Nigeria, we always packed his meals to school and added only a spoon or a fork. I started by introducing a knife to cut soft food, and he learnt this through modelling and loads of opportunities provided to practice at his own pace. Generally, for self-feeding with utensils, it was mainly consistency that helped my son learn as he built his confidence over time.

Step-by-step process

Another self-care activity we started to teach him early was dressing. It was incorporated into his potty training before he turned three years old. As part of his potty-training process, he learnt to take off and put on his pants. Also, after bath time, we involved him in dressing as much as he could handle. Taking off bottoms like trousers was easier as we modelled it and used short phrases like "pull down." Taking off tops had to be broken down using short phrases like "hands up" so he knew to raise his hands as we guided him. It took some time for him to learn to take off tops independently, especially when pulling the top over his head. He eventually got it over time as we practised so many times.

The next thing was learning how to put on his clothes. We started by placing his trousers on the floor, asked him to sit on the floor and guided him to put his legs into each trouser leg. We modelled this for a while and talked him through the process, like when he learnt to remove his clothes. After some time, he started to do it himself. We then moved to tops, this time putting it over his head initially and then guiding him to put his hand through each arm hole with short phrases like "hands in" and "pull down" to wear it fully. This also took some time, and at the beginning, he was slow at it, but we were patient on most days. On days we were in a rush, say school mornings, we were tempted to dress him up ourselves. However, we made up for it by involving him while preparing for bedtime using his pyjamas.

Teaching my son how to use zippers and buttons came after he could put on and take off his clothes independently. Pulling zippers up and down did not require much effort compared to buttons. He learnt how to do and undo buttons on shirts by placing them on a flat surface first before learning to do so on a shirt he had on. We used a combination of demonstrating and then standing in front of the mirror so he could watch himself as he did it. He did not like looking in the mirror and preferred looking down as he tried to button the shirt. Unbuttoning a shirt was what he learnt first, then buttoning. It took over a year before he learnt both independently, and he still needs help with buttons closer to his neck.

Brushing his teeth independently was the next self-care activity we tackled between four and five years old. This was tricky as my son was sensitive to anyone brushing his teeth, much less him doing so independently. He cried and sometimes shouted as we brushed his teeth. I later learnt that brushing his teeth was a sensory issue for him, so we learnt to do it with patience. The motivation for getting him to learn to brush his teeth alone was to support his independence. We used a regular toothbrush for him at this stage and started by brushing for him as before, and then we handed over the toothbrush for him to have a go. We either gave him the brush at the beginning or the end before whoever supported his brushing took over. Before we handed him the toothbrush, we would have already put toothpaste on so there would be no anxiety from needless waiting. He struggled initially, which took him some time, but we tackled it in stages. We used loads of praise to get him to try brushing independently, even if it was just for a few seconds each time. We also tried using a mirror so he could look at himself as he held the brush, but that was not always successful.

As he got more comfortable holding the toothbrush to his mouth, we guided him with phrases like "teeth together" and "tongue out" so he knew where to place the toothbrush for cleaning. We will then routinely finish up for him and rinse off. We later moved to encourage him to brush his teeth on his own the whole time as we watched and talked him through the process initially. Between these stages, we taught him how to put the toothpaste on the brush and rinse afterwards. As he got more comfortable, I started paying attention to the brushing technique and used phrases like "round and round" so he understood how to use circular motions to brush. It took about two years before we were comfortable that he could brush his teeth without us having to intervene. After he started brushing independently, we bought a two-minute sand timer to let him know how long he would spend brushing his teeth. He tended to rush, so we thought the timer would help. We stopped using the timer after a few weeks as he didn't use it consistently, so we resorted to asking him to go back and brush again if we felt he had rushed through it. We introduced an electric toothbrush; surprisingly, the vibration did not bother him. He enjoyed using the electric toothbrush and was already used to brushing his teeth independently before we switched to an electric toothbrush. The electric toothbrush helped with timing and guiding him on how long to spend brushing his teeth, as most are programmed to stay on for about two minutes. Until he was about eight years old, we either monitored him as he brushed or asked him afterwards if he had brushed all areas, like the back of the teeth, tongue, etc., to check that he had brushed correctly.

Tailored guidance

Personal hygiene activities were the trickiest, in my opinion, as we could only teach this after establishing a proper means of communicating with my son. We started personal hygiene activities well into his third year. Much like potty training, everyone in our home had to be committed to supporting my son with personal hygiene activities. Washing hands was already incorporated into his potty-training process.

Brushing his hair independently started at around six years old. Like brushing his teeth, my son was sensitive to anyone brushing his hair, as it took him a couple of years to sit still for a haircut. When I felt he was ready to start brushing his hair, around five years old, I just handed him the brush and talked him through the process. I tried different options, too, like asking him to stand in front of the mirror and watch as I brushed his hair so he could see how I did it. It took a while until we got to the stage where he could do it alone, as the sensitivity sometimes made him reluctant to try. We just encouraged him to do it anyway, even if it was to move the brush across his hair slowly. He got better with time, but even after brushing his hair himself, his dad or I still had to help him finish it as he tends to rush through it. We often helped with areas that were easy to miss, like the sides and back of the head.

We started trying to teach him to shower independently after he had mastered dressing independently. I cannot recall his exact age at the time, but he knew body parts before we started. Like other self-care activities, we demonstrated and then talked him through the process. We then gave him the sponge to try on his own several times, and then we finished up for him with rinsing off at the end. We reduced support gradually as he became confident. I was particular about technique, guiding him on how to wash each part of his body correctly, so we monitored him as he showered for some time. We withdrew monitoring after we were confident he could shower properly independently.

Taking off his shoes started alongside teaching him how to put on and remove his clothes. We didn't even need to teach this per se, as he figured it out after we asked him to a couple of times by saying, "Shoes off." Putting on shoes with straps started before he turned five years old to complement the independent dressing cycle we started earlier. Most of his shoes at this stage were Velcro-style or slip-on shoes with one or a few straps. From when he started school, they recommended Velcro-style shoes. We just stuck to buying this type of shoes for him for a long time. Putting on these styles of shoes was not particularly difficult for him to learn with continuous guidance and demonstration. We just let him do it, and on days he needed help, he asked, and we supported him till he learnt to wear them independently. The only part of the process we taught was to show him how to distinguish the left from the right shoe by correcting when he placed the shoes incorrectly.

Tying shoelaces independently happened at nine years old. Before then, we helped with tying his shoelaces. He was beginning to have more and more shoes with laces, so he had to learn to do it independently. Due to the various steps involved, I used YouTube videos to supplement guiding him. Over a summer holiday, I started by modelling and breaking the steps down using references he could remember. For instance, I associated the crossing of both ends of the laces with the letter X so he had a visual reference. I also used the phrases "push in" and "pull out" to describe the actions for tying. I consistently talked him through the process for the first few weeks as I tied the laces with his shoe on. Then, I allowed him to practice most mornings for the remainder of the holidays as I monitored and guided him where necessary. He eventually got it, albeit doing it slowly.

Routines

There is no skill my son learnt without incorporating it into his routine. We incorporated all the self-care activities he had learnt individually into his routine, and he learnt to do them in the right order with daily practice. Visual charts might have helped, but I didn't bother. I just adopted a process that he could easily do anywhere we went. We used to prompt him if he forgot to do any part of the process. For instance, if his hair was not brushed, we would remind him to go and do it. By eight years old, he was used to getting himself ready each morning and changing into pyjamas by bedtime without prompting. This was largely due to him carrying out the activities in sequence daily for many years. Once we felt he had mastered any of the self-care skills, we left him to it and monitored him periodically. We only intervened when he asked for help to build his confidence and independence.